AUTISM GIVES ME SUPERPOWERS!

PAYTON BIGGERS

Note to Readers

When Payton was eighteen months old, her pediatrician informed us that he suspected she had Asperger's. Being that she was our first and only child, my husband John and I didn't have any other children to compare her to or experiences to draw on from others around us. We knew she was highly intelligent as we'd begun teaching her to read at six months old. Before she could talk, she could read/identify 250 words. We knew that loud noises frightened her and she didn't like large crowds and that she was highly sensitive. She would play quietly, read for hours on end, and entertain herself for long periods of time. After much thought, we decided to not have her tested. We didn't want anyone (society, family, or friends) labeling her as if something was wrong with her. We made the decision to not tell her. We didn't want her to grow up thinking she had any limits.

During her toddler years, there were times we struggled. Brushing her hair, misunderstandings because she takes everything very literally, tying her shoes, and so many other things. Looking back, we would have done things differently, but at the time, we were doing what we thought was best. There were many tears shed and many feelings hurt as we learned how best to help her. Our families didn't always understand when we skipped large family gatherings, left early when she was over stimulated, and avoided stressful situations. Many family members would try to encourage her to dress and act like other children. It took time for some of them to understand, and some still don't. Many times they thought she was spoiled when we were just putting her different needs first.

Payton has always struggled to interact with kids her age and younger. In thirteen years, she has had one sleepover with friends that proved to be overwhelming. Neuro-typical kids don't always understand her and can be very cruel. They can make her uncomfortable about her vocabulary, her clothes, her interests, and so much more. And not just kids but adults too. She has been made fun of by adults as well for "having a head full of useless knowledge" or for being obsessed with a topic. Payton is one of the most fascinating people I have ever met. Her knowledge and vocabulary amaze me daily. She has the sweetest personality and the biggest heart of anyone you have ever met.

When she was two, she entered "school." It was a daycare, in essence, that also provided a K3 and K4 program. I remember her coming home one day very hungry because she didn't eat lunch and wasn't allowed a dessert or snack because she didn't eat lunch. I was furious. She wasn't refusing lunch as a misbehavior. She had sensitivities to certain foods and certain textures that literally made her gag. She physically couldn't eat her lunch that day. All I could think about was how many times would she be punished like this for something she had no control over. It was during those years that we decided to homeschool.

During the next few years, she excelled in her studies and in music and art. At a very young age, she was playing multiple musical instruments and creating amazing artwork. However, by age nine or ten, she still couldn't tie her shoes and was made fun of at times for this. She was also beginning to notice she was different and was struggling in some areas. We decided that it may be time to tell her the truth. Figuring out how was the hard part. We didn't want her to think anything was wrong with her. We wanted her to know she was special and gifted. I had been reading about Temple Grandin and saw so many similarities between her and Payton. We decided to order the book of her life. When it arrived, I explained to Payton that I wanted her to read about this amazing woman as part of school that week. Within a couple of days, Payton came into the kitchen and asked me if she was autistic. I didn't answer her directly at that time but inquired as to why she asked. She just knew from reading the story that she and Temple Grandin were the same. She was so proud. The excitement could be seen on her face. For once she didn't feel awkward or different, but instead felt special and understood why she was the way she was.

We reached out to our pediatrician and told him we wanted her evaluated so that we could address some of the areas she struggled in. He first ordered occupational therapy and also referred us to a psychologist in Atlanta who specializes in high functioning autistic girls. Occupational therapy was amazing. Within a short period of time, Payton was able to tie her shoes and her handwriting improved 100%. The small things that she had struggled with were mastered quickly.

The three of us traveled together to Atlanta for the consultation. John and I had time to speak with the doctor in private and then Payton had time as well. Payton and I then returned the next week for three days of extensive testing and evaluations, which confirmed everything we already knew but also provided us great insight into how Payton sees things. I remember Payton point blank asking the doctor, "Am I autistic?" When the doctor said, "Why yes you are," Payton's face lit up with pride. It was as if she had found her place.

I am not saying every problem was solved at that moment, but it brought us all to a greater understanding. We also learned about communicating. Payton has never been one to complain or ask for anything, but she finally began to understand that she had to be open and honest with us. We also began to learn what it means that Payton sees things in pictures. And she began to learn that we don't see things that way.

As a Christian family, we believe God does not make mistakes. He made Payton exactly the way she was intended to be. He gave her a heart of gold and the kindest soul. He gave her intelligence that I can't even begin to grasp. And He also gave her to John and me, because He knew we would protect her at all cost. The world can be cruel, adults and kids alike. It is our job to protect her and help her grow to the best of her ability. Her doctor told us once in a session that we would lose friends and family in an effort to do what was best for Payton. We initially questioned this, but we soon discovered that no truer words had ever been spoken. We have lost several close friends and family because they chose not to support her. The single most important thing parents of autistic children can do is to protect them and support them regardless of the consequences. The special friends and family who remain a part of her life have had a huge impact on her growth and positive progress.

The past three years have been much easier for our family. We all have a greater sense of understanding. We know what over stimulates her, what calms her, and what she needs on a daily basis. One example immediately comes to mind. When Payton was ten and right after her evaluation, she and I set out on a 3,000-mile road trip alone through nine states. As a travel writer, my trips are sometimes very busy with moving from place to place and event to event quickly. It can be tough at times for anyone. We were in Indiana on day twelve or thirteen of this particular trip, and I could tell Payton was over stimulated. After the second museum of the day, I knew she needed some time away from big crowds, time alone, and time to do the one activity that calms her faster than anything else. I immediately stopped what we were doing and pulled up google maps. I found a playground just two blocks away that had swings. As soon as she saw them, her face lit up! After about twenty to thirty minutes on the swing, she was feeling much better. Traveling is one of Payton's favorite things to do, but I have to keep in mind that she also needs time to do the things that are important to her wellbeing.

So why did Payton write this book, and why are we telling you all of this? To help others. Should we have told Payton at a young age that she was on the spectrum? Maybe. Would it have changed anything? Probably. John and I don't have any regrets on our decisions because we have done everything in what we thought was her best interest. However, knowing some of the things that she has written in this book many years ago would have definitely made things easier along the way. We are hoping that kids on the spectrum will read this book and better understand some of the things they are going through. And to also see that they are special. As Temple Grandin's mother once said, "Different, not less." We also want typical kids and their parents to read this book and think about how they treat people who are different. We can all do better at accepting the fact that our differences are what makes each of us unique. I know without a doubt that Payton makes the world a better place every day and is going to do amazing things. Will she go to college? Get married? Have a family? Or any of the other typical things society thinks she should do? We have no idea. But I do know she will be a good person and her dad and I will do everything we can to help her become the person she was meant to be.

We ask you to take your time reading her book and really feel the emotion she put into every word and drawing. All of the illustrations are her own, and I believe that if you look deeply, you will see her feelings and heart in every one of them. After reading this book, you may wonder how she came up with the title. It is simple. After discovering her place on the spectrum, she has been able to accept who she is and begin to discover all of the superpowers she has been given. If you are special enough to be on the spectrum with her, we challenge you to find your superpowers and use them to make the world a better place.

I don't like having my hair brushed. It feels like it's pulling my hair out! Because my head is very sensitive and I don't like it being brushed too hard. I prefer to do it myself.

I don't like a lot of loud noises going on at once.

Lots of people talking and laughing really loudly.

bright lights. and loud music all at once is overstimulating.

Loud music.
Bright lights.
Loud laughing.
Many people talking.

I have a lot of trouble communicating and dealing
with little kids, mostly ones under 5 years old.

They often say things that make no sense
They often do things that make me cringe.
They can be messy.
They can be loud.

I'm very sensitive to tone of voice,

like if someone seems angry or stern,

and I don't like being yelled at.

It scares me.

I often like to dress a little differently from other people.

I prefer nicer clothes over casual clothes.

and I don't really follow fashion trends.

I often talk to myself, which bothers a lot of people.

I daydream all the time, which makes me say things to myself,

and some people are quite unsettled by that.

I really don't know why.

Stop talking to yourself!
It's weird!!!

I often don't understand sarcastic terms of speech.

Sometimes those sayings and figures of speech are confusing to me.

Time flies when you're having fun.
? ? ?
It's time to let the cat out of the bag.

A lot of times when I'm overstimulated.
I like to get on my swing set. since I like the rhythmic motion.
Is there anything that helps you?

I often struggle with timers

because I focus more on it than the work I'm given.

and I can get really worried about it.

I like to listen to music on my headphones,

overstimulated or not.

I am often obsessed with one or a few specific topics.

Sharks.

Presidents.

Mythology.

Other stories I am writing.

Sharks
Presidents
Mythology

I prefer to read than watch TV.
TV is kind of boring!

I dislike the textures of certain foods,

such as most cooked vegetables

and some types of gravy.

When I was younger,

things that are often considered easy were difficult for me,

and things that are often considered difficult were easier for me.

For instance, I learned to play the violin

years before I learned to tie my shoes.

Communication is very important.
You should talk with your friends and family
about things that bother you, like loud sounds, certain smells,
particular food textures, stressful situations, etc.
But I'll warn you: sometimes it may not work.
The person may think you're making excuses or talking back.
If this happens, try talking to him or her again later
until you can reach an understanding.

And even if you are autistic,
that's completely okay!
There's nothing wrong with it!
You can do anything!
Be yourself!
Don't change anything or hide who you are!

Advice for Non-Autistic Children

Be kind and understanding. There are some situations when understanding means more than anything. Don't exclude an autistic boy or girl from fun activities just because of how they act, and never laugh at them or make fun of them. Be accommodating, just as each and every individual needs others to be accommodating of their differences no matter how big or small those differences are.

Don't play your music too loudly, don't force eye contact, and please don't play with your toys too loudly or continue on when the girl or boy is overstimulated. Listen to them talk about their special interests. It might be fascinating, and you might become interested too!

Most importantly, if you have an autistic brother or sister, *please do not ever* say things like, "I wish I didn't have an autistic sister/brother." Or "It would be nice not having an autistic brother/sister." How would you feel if one of your siblings basically said they wish you never existed?

Please remember these things.

Advice for Parents, Teachers, Caretakers, Friends/Family, Other Adults

Being autistic is a great thing. It makes a boy or girl unique. As a parent or other kind of special adult, you want to accommodate the child, however old he or she is. Certain parenting styles may not work for an autistic person. And don't listen to people who tell you that taking your child to an aquarium and getting them marine encyclopedias to support their special interest on oceans, or anything like that, is spoiling them and not good parenting. You should do what is best for your person and encourage their interests rather than go along with what everyone else thinks.

Also, whether your autistic son/daughter is nonverbal or not, please—*pretty please*—don't talk about him or her as if he or she is not in the room. Your child is listening. It might hurt their feelings and affect them in the future.

Never, ever, record an autistic person when he or she is having a meltdown. They likely don't want a moment of their distress posted online and then having to endure other people judging them and/or making fun of them anymore than you would.

Also, one very important thing to keep in mind is to never make an autistic person act neurotypical. Don't force her or him to eat foods with textures they don't like or to wear clothes that make them uncomfortable. Don't force eye contact, make them hide over stimulation, make them not talk about their special interests, or intentionally put them in stressful environments so they can "recover from autism." Instead, change yourself. You shouldn't expect an autistic person to behave and experience life the same way you do. It's your responsibility to figure out how you can accommodate them and better understand them in any way possible. Whether it's figuring out what noises are painful, what textures are gross, what environments are stressful, anything.

And, if your daughter or son is overstimulated or having a meltdown, *please* do not use restraints. Just don't. Not even the 'humane' ones. Restraints can make the situation way worse and cause them a lot of pain, physically and emotionally. Even if the person is self-harming, things like occupational therapy (which helped me tremendously with lots of things) can help with this. One thing I would recommend when a person is overstimulated or having a meltdown is asking her or him what can help, whether it is a hug, a weighted blanket, a weighted vest, listening to music, playing with a fidget toy, having a stuffed animal, being in a quiet space, etc. Getting their input on their needs can clear up a lot of misunderstandings.

Things you can do to help are: listen to their special interests (it might be interesting), don't speak in a stern voice around them unless it is absolutely necessary, don't prevent stimming (unless the person is self-harming), don't punish them for being overstimulated or having a meltdown, and, most importantly, *please* be understanding and accommodating even if it's something like letting the autistic person watch their favorite episode on TV at 5:30 every afternoon, take a shower at 6:00 p.m. every evening, have a specific routine for getting up and getting ready for bed, not stay up past midnight, or always drinking a glass of milk before bed. Let them do these things. Routines are soothing.

People who don't know much about autism might give you unsolicited advice such as information about diets that can make autism go away or a medication that can reduce autistic traits. Always consider the source. They may be well intentioned, but even the best intentions that have no basis in fact just are not helpful. Appreciate their efforts but get advice from reliable sources.

For both parents and non-parents, when your kid gets their autism diagnosis, don't act like it's the end of the world. No matter where they are on the spectrum, they can still do things a neurotypical person can do, such as living on their own, having a job, getting married, having children or grandchildren, and being successful. Did you know that some of the smartest people who changed the world were autistic?

One last piece of advice: autistic people prefer the term 'autistic' instead of 'has autism.'

Please, remember these things.

Sincerely,

Payton

Join the Biggers family as they explore the world with the goal of showing Payton all 50 states and as many countries as possible before she turns 18.
https://endlessfamilytravels.com/autism-friendly-holidays-vacations/